TYING THE
KNOT *TIGHTER*

TYING THE
KNOT *TIGHTER*

Because Marriage Lasts a Lifetime

MARTHA PEACE
AND
JOHN CROTTS

PUBLISHING
P.O. BOX 817 • PHILLIPSBURG • NEW JERSEY 08865-0817

Printed in the United States of America

Library of Congress Cataloging-in-Publication Data

Peace, Martha.
  Tying the knot tighter : because marriage lasts a lifetime / Martha Peace and John Crotts.
     p. cm.
  Includes bibliographical references.
  ISBN-13: 978-1-59638-074-5 (pbk.)
  1. Marriage—Biblical teaching. 2. Marriage—Religious aspects—Christianity—Textbooks. I. Crotts, John, 1968- II. Title.
  BS680.M35P43 2007
  248.8'44—dc22

                              2007026242

This book is dedicated to four couples who love the Lord, love each other, and love us!

Martha's children and their spouses:

Anna and Tony Maupin
David and Jaimee Peace

John's parents and brother and his spouse:

John and Jane Crotts
Jeff and Judy Crotts

Contents

CONTENTS

Acknowledgments

This book was John Crotts's idea, and he was so enthusiastic about it that I readily agreed to write it with him. It was a joy working with John because he is humble and because he helps me with theology and some of the finer points of grammar. Another person who was a joy to work with was my daughter, Anna Maupin. Anna faithfully edited each chapter, listened to our thoughts, waded through our fuzzy, vague sentences, and fixed it all. Also many thanks to Marvin Padgett and Eric Anest from P&R Publishing for their help and guidance on this project. By the way, while in the process of editing this book, Eric got married!

MARTHA PEACE

My wife, Lynn, who used to be a professional proofreader, somehow managed to proofread our manuscript in between homeschooling three daughters and expecting a fourth baby, a boy! In addition, I want to thank Faith

9

Bible Church. You make my job a joy, and you were the first ones to receive all of these essentials.

JOHN CROTTS

The Lord is the one to whom we are both most grateful. Truly, he is awesome, and we love him. May he use this book in your life for his glory and your good.

Introduction

*L*ynn is tired as she happily packs our suitcases. In addition to our clothes and necessities, she includes our Bibles, the budget, and a couple of helpful Christian books. We are leaving for our annual marriage retreat. After we drop off the kids and the rabbit at the home of friends, the two of us drive to a cozy cabin in the mountains of north Georgia for a couple of nights. These retreats have proven to be sweet times of rest when we refocus our priorities, adjust our budget, agree on family goals, have fun, and encourage one another in our walks with Christ.

Taking time apart to refresh ourselves on the foundations of marriage is vital for success as a couple. This is true for all Christian marriages. Just as the best players never get past the basics of their sport, so Christian couples need to be regularly reminded of the basics of a Christian marriage. This book sets out to provide such reminders. It assumes you have some Bible background or have access to other resources to fill in what you are lacking. We have identified nineteen areas of marriage, summarized the Bible's teaching, and then offered a series of penetrating questions to help you take inventory of yourself and your marriage. Each section ends with a couple of the best resources we know to dig deeper in that area.

Ways to Use This Book

In addition to serving as a resource for a marriage retreat, this book can be used in many different ways. Any time of the year is a great time to get back to basics. Your wedding anniversary might be such a time. Or, couples could read a chapter a night or one per week for a quick refresher in one facet of their marriage. (The chapter on sex might even extend the evening!)

Also, a mentoring couple could work through this material with a young couple from church. Although this book could be used as a supplement to premarital counseling, it's probably too brief to be the main resource. That being said, a pastor or counselor could use the book to guide a more in-depth discussion. Certainly, any marriage counselees could be directed to the chapters about areas in which they are struggling. Many men and women who have been well taught need only to be reminded of the Bible's plain teaching to be quickly realigned with God's design. An honest heart-to-heart talk focused on the right things is often an astounding eye-opener for couples.

How to Get the Most Out of the Book

Even though the chapters are short and are written in a conversational tone, the message of each section strives to capture the heart of the Bible's teaching on the specific area of Christian marriage. You and your spouse will experience the maximum benefit of this book by considering the following advice.

First, read each section carefully. The goal is not to get through the book as fast as you can. Your heart's desire should be to please the Lord. The wisdom contained in these pages is God's truth from his Word. As a tea bag transforms steaming water, God's transforming Word can saturate your soul. Writing down a few notes can be a helpful way of slowing down the process of reading. If you think of related verses or principles not mentioned in the chapter, jot them down. Writing down your questions will also motivate you to seek out the answers.

Second, take the application questions seriously. In a longer list of questions it is easy to skim over the harder ones. Again, writing out the answers in a notebook could be useful. This would be especially true if you and your spouse are reading the book separately. Comparing notes is easier than trying to remember all of your thoughts from the previous week.

As we tell those we minister to, the more effort you put into your answers, the more you and your marriage will benefit. Thoughtless answers to important questions could prove to be more harmful than helpful. Ask the Lord to show you your hearts. Ask him to help you be honest and thorough in your answers. Even though it could be painful, you will never be able to repent about that which you never see or admit. The doctor can't cure what is never diagnosed.

Humble your heart as you share your answers with your spouse. Make it easy for him or her to offer insights that you may have missed about your marriage, even if those insights reveal your failures. There is no virtue in bringing in an inspector just to scan the surface but ignore the potentially serious structural flaws. What does it profit to pass an inspection only to have the building collapse later? Listen to the wisdom of Proverbs 9:7–9:

> Whoever corrects a scoffer gets himself abuse,
>   and he who reproves a wicked man incurs injury.
> Do not reprove a scoffer, or he will hate you;
>   reprove a wise man, and he will love you.
> Give instruction to a wise man, and he will be still wiser;
>   teach a righteous man, and he will increase in
>   learning.

Third, search out the resources for digging deeper. As we have said, this book scratches the surface; the books and booklets we recommend go much deeper. If one or two of the chapters in this book reveal shortcomings in your marriage, take the time to work through the more thorough studies of the Bible on the matters, and get help when it is needed. Our marriages are gifts from the Lord. They are worth the additional investment!

Because marriage lasts a lifetime, our prayer is that the Lord will be at work in your hearts as you remember the essentials of a Christian marriage and carefully examine your lives in light of the Scriptures. Repent where you need to. Encourage or comfort each other where you need to. Always look to the Lord and his beautiful work on the cross for the grace of forgiveness for failures, as well as the motivation to grow and change.

BASICS

I

Love for the Lord

Remember when you and your spouse were dating? Way back when you couldn't wait to hear the telephone ring or for the evening to hurry up and arrive so that you could be together on your date? You thought about what you would wear and how long it would take you to get ready. You desired each other above all others. You yearned for the day when you could be husband and wife and be together so much more of the time. You longed for that day because you loved and desired each other.

But a Christian has someone else to long for, desire, and love even more than a husband or wife. That someone else is, of course, our Lord Jesus Christ.

Even "though you have not seen him, you love him" (1 Peter 1:8). We do not see him now because he is in heaven in all his glory and majesty. Listen to the psalmist Asaph's eloquent words:

Whom have I in heaven but you?
>And there is nothing on earth that I desire besides
>>you.

My flesh and my heart may fail,
>but God is the strength of my heart and my portion
>>forever.

For behold, those who are far from you shall perish;
>you put an end to everyone who is unfaithful to you.

But for me it is good to be near God;
>I have made the Lord GOD my refuge,
>that I may tell of all your works. (Ps. 73:25–28)

The most important relationship that anyone will ever have is the relationship with the Lord, and your love for him is the most basic expression of what it means to be a Christian. Those who love the Lord have a hunger and thirst to be righteous as he is righteous. They are grateful to him as well as obedient. They trust the Lord and love not only him but also their brothers in Christ.

A desire for and love for the Lord are paramount for husband and wife if they are going to have a marriage that glorifies God. If they do not love the Lord, then they cannot love each other as God intends. What about you and your marriage? Think about that as you consider the following questions.

QUESTIONS FOR REFLECTION AND APPLICATION

⚑ Are you confident that you have placed your faith in Christ and Christ alone?

❧ Do you think about the Lord often throughout your day?

❧ Do you talk to him in your heart (in your mind)?

❧ Is your heart for the Lord apparent to those who know you well?

❧ Do you love the Lord even above your family?

❧ Is your life marked more by trusting God or by worrying?

❧ Is your life characterized by obedience to the Scriptures?

❧ Do you look forward to what God is going to do in your life?

❧ If we could ask the Lord, would he say that you are a grateful child?

❧ Is your obedience to the Lord Jesus motivated by joy?

❧ What are some ways your love for God trickles over into your relationship with your spouse?

FAVORITE RESOURCES

J. I. Packer. *Knowing God.* Downers Grove, IL: InterVarsity Press, 1973.

Maurice Roberts. *The Thought of God.* Edinburgh: The Banner of Truth Trust, 1993.

Our gracious, holy Lord,

The only reason that we can love you is because you first loved us.

When we think of you dying in our place and cleansing us of our sin, we cannot help but bow down and worship you.

We are so grateful.

Give us the heart of the psalmist who desired nothing on earth besides you.

Help us to be mindful of you throughout our day.

Help us to show our love to you by being grateful, obedient children.

Because you first loved us, we ask these things.

Amen.

2

Bible Reading

artha's daughter, Anna, has five children, and the two youngest are boys. Matthew is barely three, and Noah is one-and-a-half. It is always interesting to eat a meal with the two of them. Matthew is too busy to sit down and eat a meal. He will play with his food, play with the person beside him, or beg to get down from the table after three or four bites. You often hear someone say, "Matthew, EAT!" Noah, by contrast, loves to eat. He will eat everything in sight and is almost as big as Matthew even though he is younger. It seems that the more Noah eats, the more he wants. Matthew does not desire to eat much because other things are much more important to him.

Reading the Bible can be like Matthew's appetite (not really hungry, easily distracted) or like Noah's appetite (can't wait to eat, the more the better). Just as Noah eats his food, so husbands and wives should regularly and consistently feed on God's Word. God's Word should be like a precious treasure;

Scripture itself reminds us, "like newborn infants, long for the pure spiritual milk, that by it you may grow up to salvation" (1 Peter 2:2).

The more you read, meditate on, and memorize Scripture, the greater your desire will grow for more. In fact, it should be such a treasure for us that we have an attitude like Job's: he "treasured the words of [God's] mouth more than [his own] portion of food" (Job 23:12).

The importance of Bible reading cannot be overstated, for all Scriptures were given for our instruction and are profitable to teach as well as reprove us. In addition, Christians are to feed on God's Word and know Scripture so that they won't be deceived by false teaching.

The psalmist tells us that we gain understanding from God's Word, and that Word gives us wisdom. Reading the Scriptures is one way that God's Word abides in us. Since growing in the knowledge of our Lord is a command (2 Peter 3:18), reading the Bible should be a priority and regular discipline in the life of every husband and wife. What about you? Are you more like Matthew, who picks at his food, or like Noah, who delights in eating? Think about your life and your priorities as you consider the following questions.

QUESTIONS FOR REFLECTION AND APPLICATION

- How much time do you spend per day reading the Scriptures?
- Is daily Bible reading part of your regular routine?
- What time of day would most likely result in your reading Scripture consistently?
- Have you read the entire Bible?

- ❧ Is reading the Bible such a priority in your life that you are willing to get up earlier or willing to go to bed earlier so that you will be fresh and alert the next day to read your Bible?
- ❧ If you do not have time to read your Bible, do you have time to watch television?
- ❧ Do you sometimes journal about what God is teaching you through his Word?
- ❧ When convicted about sin in your life, do you focus on specific Scriptures to help you change by God's grace?
- ❧ Do you know the Scriptures well enough that you would not be deceived by false teachers?
- ❧ Do you and your spouse ever read Scripture together?
- ❧ Is Scripture where you and your spouse turn to answer life's questions?

FAVORITE RESOURCES

Wayne Mack and Joshua Mack. *The Twin Pillars of the Christian Life.* Sand Spring, OK: Grace and Truth Books, 2003.

Richard Mayhue. *How to Interpret the Bible for Yourself.* Fearn, Ross-Shire, Scotland: Christian Focus, 1997.

Our wise and abundantly merciful God,

How astonishing it is that you have given us your Word and that every word is true as well as powerful.

You are the one who illuminates our minds by the truths of Scripture.

Through your Word, you warn us and give us wisdom, and we grow in Christlikeness.

Place in our hearts a longing for your Word that is as great the baby's longing for his mother's milk.

Give us such a desire for the Scriptures that no matter how much we learn, we will only desire more.

We ask this for your glory and in Jesus' name,

Amen.

3

A Person of Prayer

The adage says, "The family that prays together stays together." Although that is true to a degree, the family that prays together must be grounded upon a husband and wife who pray alone! If you are to be the best spouse that you can be, you must be a person of prayer.

Prayer keeps your priorities in line. When all is said and done, the dishes can wait, the lawn can wait, but your relationship with God cannot wait. Prayer is an acknowledgment that you aren't the perfect spouse! You need God's help. God uses prayer to change you into the man or woman he wants you to be.

As with exercise, *consistency* in prayer is better than a big burst every couple of weeks. Spiritual growth requires a good habit of daily prayer. The Bible says that we are to "pray without ceasing" (1 Thess. 5:17). You don't have to pray for long periods of time for it to be beneficial, but you do have to seek the Lord consistently. Create a prayer plan—record it in a notebook, in your computer or PDA, or on index cards to have before you.

There are many different kinds of prayer in the Bible. The Psalms, in particular, include expressions of praise, thanksgiving, confession of sins, and love for and trust in the Lord. All of these areas can be included within your prayer plan. For example, you could choose a different attribute of God for which to praise him each day of the week. In addition to these types of prayer, make sure your plan includes some specific personal concerns for which to seek God's help.

PRAYING FOR YOURSELF

It is vital to pray for yourself. Better than anyone else, you know how far you have to go in becoming a godly husband or wife. Seek God's powerful help! Ask him to make you godly, wise, better in your marriage role, compassionate, holy, and humble. Identify your weak spots, and then target them for prayer. Ask your spouse what areas he or she thinks you need to work on, and then lift those things to the Lord.

> Search me, O God, and know my heart!
>> Try me and know my thoughts!
> And see if there be any grievous way in me,
>> and lead me in the way everlasting! (Ps. 139:23–24)

An example of an area to pray about is pride. (If you doubt this applies to you, you probably need extra help!) How many ways would your marriage improve if you were less selfish and more humble? You can be sure you are praying according to the heart of God when you seek him for humility. He will love to answer your prayer because "God opposes the proud but gives grace to the humble" (1 Peter 5:5). Your life will be changed, and your marriage will be changed, all because you prayed about your pride.

Praying for Your Spouse

Praying for your spouse is a wonderful way to fulfill your role in the home. A husband is taking spiritual responsibility for his family as he lifts them before God's throne. A wife is giving her husband tremendous spiritual help as she intercedes for her man.

You can't change your spouse—but God can. It is vital to pray for him or her. Target those areas in which your spouse needs to grow. Share with one another your burdens and your weak spots. Be sure to also thank God for your spouse. Get specific. Every good gift is from God. Thank God for each of your spouse's virtues.

Praying for Your Children

If the Lord has blessed you with children, be sure to make them special objects of prayer. Seek the Lord for their salvation. Ask him to give them godly Christian character. Pray that they will honor and obey you, and pray that you will have grace to nurture and admonish them in the Lord. While you don't know the identity of their future spouse, God does. Be sure to ask him for a good spouse for your child.

Praying together and staying together truly are great. But to give the maximum benefit to your family, be sure to be a person of prayer by yourself as well. As you seek God, you will become more like him. As you become more like him, your life and your marriage will be transformed!

Questions for Reflection and Application

- ❧ Do you pray?
- ❧ How many days per week do you pray at least fifteen minutes?
- ❧ How many days in a row have you last prayed?
- ❧ Is there variety in your prayers?
- ❧ What are some areas to praise God for?
- ❧ What can you thank God for?
- ❧ Do you have sins that need to be confessed to God?
- ❧ What are the areas of struggle that you most need to pray about?
- ❧ What would your spouse say are your or his or her areas of struggle?
- ❧ What are you thankful for about your spouse?
- ❧ Do you pray for your children by name each day?
- ❧ Are you praying in faith that God can and will answer your prayers in accordance with his will?

Favorite Resources

J. C. Ryle. *Call to Prayer.* Laurel, MS: Audubon Press and Charles Nolan Publishers, 2002. (reprinted ed.)

John MacArthur. *Lord, Teach Me to Pray.* Nashville: J. Countryman, 2003.

Father, you are such a wonderful and gracious God!

I am amazed that you have granted me access into your very presence through the work of Jesus.

Help me to pray.

Help me to seek you about my shortcomings and those of my spouse and my children.

More than anything, Father, give me a heart to be in your presence.

Fill me with such amazement with your love and mercy toward me that I can't wait to be with you again and again.

In the name of the provider of my right of entry, Jesus Christ,

Amen.

4

Your Family in God's Family

You were never meant to grow as a Christian all alone. Nor were you intended to mature as a Christian couple in isolation. For you to be all that you can be as an individual believer and as a couple, your family must be vitally linked with a local expression of God's family.

The church is near and dear to the heart of God. In 1 Timothy 3:15, Paul calls the church "the household of God, which is the church of the living God, a pillar and buttress of truth." A church is an expression of God's household, God's possession, with a serious responsibility to uphold God's truth in the world. In other places, the Bible calls the church the "body of Christ" (1 Cor. 12:27) and says that it was purchased with Christ's blood (Acts 20:28).

God designed individual Christians to function sur-
rounded by a variety of other Christians—young, old, single,
those with large families, rich, poor, more and less mature, and
so on. The picture of one body with many parts (1 Cor. 12)
displays God's intention. No matter what you have to offer,
you were crafted to play a part within a church family. As one
part of the body, you, with your gifts and abilities, are critical
to the success of the whole, and you need the rest of the body
to accomplish God's design. Christians are interdependent.

Do you know there are more than forty-five commands in
the New Testament that you cannot fulfill by yourself? Each
command includes the phrase "one another." You are com-
manded to love, serve, admonish, and encourage one another.
Hebrews 10:24–25, which is often cited as the major command to be an active participant in a church family, exhorts,
"And let us consider how to stir up one another to love and
good works, not neglecting to meet together, as is the habit of
some, but encouraging one another, and all the more as you
see the Day drawing near." There is no way to fulfill any of
these commands by yourself. They were not designed to be
fulfilled merely within the confines of your home either. If
you want to honor God in your relationship with your spouse,
your family needs to be a vital part of a local church!

You and your household will find incredible personal
blessings through your participation in God's household. The
church is led by a team of godly men. These elders provide
you with instruction, accountability, counsel, example, and
leadership. In addition, Titus 2 instructs older women in the
church to teach younger women in all kinds of practical matters. The other family members will be a constant source of

blessing and encouragement as the body builds itself more and more in Christian maturity (Eph. 4:11–16).

Some couples justify staying in a bad church in order to have a good influence. But what happens when *you* have spiritual needs? How will you be able to keep growing if you are not being fed? Who is going to help you in the dark days of trial? Who will be a godly example to your children? Who will have the courage, concern, and capability to confront you or your spouse if you plunge into sin?

No church is perfect. Each one of us has the responsibility to make the church we are a part of as biblical as possible. But for you and your family to flourish, find and join the best church you can and serve the Lord there with all of your heart.

QUESTIONS FOR REFLECTION AND APPLICATION

❧ What are the marks of a good church?
❧ Can you support your answer with Scripture?
❧ Are you members of such a church?
❧ What are the ways you and your spouse are participating as part of the church family?
❧ Do you minister together? separately?
❧ Who are two couples in the church that you look to as models of godliness?
❧ When have you last invited them to your home?
❧ Who are two couples in your church that need your example?
❧ When have you last invited them to your home?
❧ What are the ways you are learning God's Word from the church?

- Are you so busy serving that you are not being spiritually fed?
- What are ways you are using your spiritual gifts through your church?
- Do you love and serve others in your church?
- Are you instilling a love for the church in your children?

FAVORITE RESOURCES

Wayne Mack and David Swavely. *Life in the Father's House.* 2nd ed. Phillipsburg, NJ: P&R Publishing, 2006.

Donald Whitney. *Spiritual Disciplines Within the Church.* Chicago: Moody Press, 1996.

Father, you have made the church to be your Son's bride.

Thank you so much for giving us the privilege of joining in your grand design.

Let us not be contented with mere attendance.

Give us a heart to join the worship of our Lord Jesus with brothers and sisters in the church family.

Give us opportunities to build up those around us to be more like Jesus.

May our church become a base for shining the light of Jesus to our community and to the world.

For the glory of Jesus we ask these things!

Amen.

5

Growing Together

Marriage provides incredible opportunities for two people to grow as Christians. The intimacy of a husband and a wife unlocks doors that can be utilized for mutual benefits. No one will ever know you better than your spouse will. No one will appreciate your spiritual strengths, and no one will experience you at your worst more than your spouse will. He or she even knows how and when you are tempted.

At our best, that means we can help get each other through the spiritually tough times—for example, with a promise from the Bible at the end of a tough day. At our worst, that means we know exactly how to push each other's buttons! Instead of provoking each other, use the countless opportunities and resources the Lord has blessed you with as a Christian couple to grow, grow, grow!

FAMILY WORSHIP

Family worship can be as simple as reading a portion of the Bible at the dinner table, singing a Christian song, and praying together. Consistency is more important than the length of time or even the depth of material covered. Find a time when you are usually together (for our family it is dinnertime). Leave a Bible on the table with a bookmark in it. Purpose to read a little each time you're together.

PRAYING TOGETHER

We've already seen the benefits of a person's individual prayer life on his or her marriage. But, as two people draw near to God together, they discover that they are also drawing closer to each other at the same time.

Seek to develop the habit of regularly asking each other for prayer requests. Although you should try to be faithful to continually pray for each other in private, sometimes it is wise to stop and spend a moment or two with the Lord in prayer right there. God has told us to be "casting all [our] anxieties on him, because he cares for [us]" (1 Peter 5:7). The cares of couples can weigh a family down. Take advantage of the Lord's offer to unload those cares on his strong shoulders.

CHECKING IN

Too many couples do their spiritual growing in isolation from each other. Take time to check in with each other. What is your husband reading in his Bible lately? Who is your wife meeting with for spiritual encouragement? Is your spouse reading a helpful book? Should you find some time to read it after he or she is finished?

Is this about accountability? Partly, but it ought to be far more than nudging each other to be more faithful. Hebrews 3:13 commands all of us, "Exhort one another every day, as long as it is called 'today,' that none of you may be hardened by the deceitfulness of sin." The command was issued to a group of persecuted people who were being tempted to turn away from Jesus. The verse also shows, however, that our hearts are like modeling clay—they dry up and get hard if they don't receive the daily water of encouragement, comfort, or exhortation.

Never allow the busyness of life to crowd out time to talk together about the things of the Lord. The world, the flesh, and the devil (not to mention the screaming infant) will oppose any such discussions. Fight back! It's worth the efforts to check in with your spouse. How can you fulfill your family roles as leader or helper if you don't share your spiritual life with each other?

MINISTERING TOGETHER

There are plenty of opportunities to serve the Lord. It is fair to say that every person you see in church represents an opportunity for service. Many families, however, become fragmented as they pour out their ministry energy in different directions.

Serving the Lord in different ministries is not wrong and is sometimes necessary, but also look for ways to serve him together. Because most couples have different gifts, talents, and desires, consider creatively seeking out or making ways to utilize each of your strengths by serving together. Neither should be selfish, but the wife also has the special consideration of being her husband's helper and glory (1 Cor. 11:7).

Such service might bring out some spiritual strengths or weaknesses that had been previously hidden from each other, providing still more opportunities to encourage or challenge your spouse and grow together.

Questions for Reflection and Application

- Do you have regular family worship in your home?
- Are you praying with your spouse?
- What are the prayer requests most near to your spouse's heart?
- When was the last time you checked in with each other spiritually?
- Are there areas in which your spouse needs comfort? encouragement? challenge?
- What books has your spouse been reading?
- Do you ever read a book together and discuss it as you go through it?
- What are some opportunities where you can serve the Lord together as a couple?

Favorite Resources

Jerry Bridges. *Growing Your Faith.* Colorado Springs, CO: NavPress, 2004.

Jerry Marcellino. *Rediscovering the Lost Treasure of Family Worship.* Laurel, MS: Audubon Press, 1996.

What a gift you gave to me, Father, when you gave me my spouse!

You knew that I would need amazing amounts of help to best follow you on the earth.

Of all of the ways you could bring me along, you choose this wonderfully wise means. Thank you!

Please, help me to be humble as my spouse helps me to grow in your grace.

Please, help me to be a good helper for my spouse to grow in grace.

Help us to glorify you better together than we ever could apart.

Amen!

ROLES

6

A Loving Leader

The Bible says that husbands are to lead their families. A wrong understanding of leadership, however, can be misleading! Autocratically barking out orders from a fluffy throne in front of the TV is not the biblical vision of a godly husband.

The main command for husbands in the primary passage about marriage roles is not to lead your wife—that's assumed. The main command is to love your wife. Ephesians 5:25 says, "Husbands, love your wives, as Christ loved the church and gave himself up for her."

Puppy love and infatuation need not apply for the fulfillment of this kind of love. Romantic feelings are important, but honeymoon fireworks last little more than two years without self-conscious hard work. Real biblical love flows from warm, unselfish thoughts toward your wife. These thoughts kindle into flames of loving attitudes. As a result, actions of self-sacrificial service will follow. Meanwhile, loving feelings will intermingle throughout the process.

Passivity and indulgence are two other imitators of biblical love that fail to measure up to the real thing. You are the leader of your home. "Wives, submit to your own husbands, as to the Lord. For the husband is the head of the wife even as Christ is the head of the church, his body, and is himself its Savior" (Eph. 5:22–23). The command to love your wife does not undo the fact of your headship; it gives your leadership its direction. Choosing to keep the peace by always doing things her way is not leadership, and it is really not loving either.

In a sense, the opposite of real love is not hatred but selfishness. Jesus' example of love is completely giving his life on the cross to meet the real needs of his people by atoning for their sins. Husband, you are called to serve your wife, to help shoulder her burdens. You should be striving to meet her real biblical needs. Sometimes that means confronting her sin or holding her accountable to change an area of struggle. A loving leader will not wimp out but will speak the truth in a loving way.

Later in Ephesians 5, Paul describes love in plain terms. "In the same way husbands should love their wives as their own bodies. He who loves his wife loves himself. For no one ever hated his own flesh, but nourishes and cherishes it, just as Christ does the church" (Eph. 5:28–29). As a giant athlete gingerly takes care of himself after an injury, so you should tenderly nourish and cherish your wife. Some of the ways you can do this are by speaking kindly to her and about her, looking at her with affection, and holding doors open for her.

When you do these things, Paul reminds you that you yourself are the ultimate beneficiary.

Some men read Ephesians 5 and suppose that as long as they are willing to literally die for their wives, if needed, they are fulfilling the command to love their wives as Christ loves his church. The only death that needs to take place in many homes today is that of the man-sized ego. Yes, you are the leader. But God clearly calls you to lead in a Christlike, loving manner—a complete death to unloving selfishness. Sometimes, you need to turn off the television and go change a diaper.

QUESTIONS FOR REFLECTION AND APPLICATION

- Are you intentionally thinking about ways to love your wife?
- Are you seeking the Lord's help in loving one of his creatures in the way he wants you to?
- What are ways you are striving to show her your love?
- When are you most tempted to be selfish at home?
- Stop and repent of ways you have been selfish. Confess those sins to the Lord and to your wife.
- What are some specific areas where you have made sacrifices because you love your wife?
- Have you let wrong ideas about love neuter your leadership?
- Does your leadership in the home reflect Christ's loving motivation and manner?
- Will you lovingly confront your wife's sin and help her to change?
- Will you write out ten loving thoughts about your wife?

❧ Will you write out ten loving actions you can do for your wife?

❧ Will you prioritize and do these things, asking the Holy Spirit to help you obey the foremost command in the main passage about your role as a husband—to love your wife?

Favorite Resources

John MacArthur. *The Fulfilled Family.* Nashville: Nelson Books, 2005.

Wayne Mack. *Strengthening Your Marriage.* Phillipsburg, NJ: P&R Publishing, 1977.

You, O Lord, know how challenging it is to love a bride.

Your life was a life of service, and your death was the ultimate sacrifice.

Thank you for your love for me even as part of that bride.

Thank you for suffering the punishment that I deserve for my failures to love my wife in the ways that you have called me to do.

Overwhelm me with your sunshine of grace, that my selfishness might melt away completely and that I might better love my wife.

For the sake of Jesus I ask these things.

Amen.

7

Wife, Love Your Husband

Weddings can be large and grand or small and simple. I recently heard of one wedding in which the three-year-old ring bearer was following his sister, the flower girl, down the aisle. His mother repeatedly reminded him, "Follow the flowers." His sister gracefully walked down the aisle sprinkling her petals on one side of the aisle and then the other. Everyone smiled as the ring bearer dutifully zigzagged down the aisle following those flowers! The adorable ring bearer was soon forgotten, however, when the bride and her father came in the room. All eyes focused on her as she walked toward her groom, and all ears strained to hear her as she repeated her vows before God and before the witnesses. Perhaps with tears in her eyes the bride vows to love her groom "till death do us part."

You probably remember making a similar vow, but you may or may not always feel as if you are living up to your vow now. Whether you feel like it or not, though, doesn't matter. What does matter is that you love your husband. Three Greek words for love help us appreciate the ways wives should love their husbands. The Greek words are *agape,* love that is sacrificial; *philos,* love that is thinking of your husband as a dear, cherished friend; and *eros,* love that is physical intimacy.

Agape love is how all Christians are to love one another. The Lord Jesus said in Matthew 22:39, "You shall love your neighbor as yourself." Your husband is your closest neighbor, and some of the practical ways you can show him love in an *agape* sense are by being patient, kind, unselfish, not jealous, rejoicing in the truth instead of unrighteousness, not being rude or provoked, and not taking into account a wrong suffered (1 Cor. 13:4–7).

Agape love is also the self-sacrificing love of our Lord Jesus for us when he died on the cross. It is the "for God so loved the world" love (John 3:16). Our Lord was *the* perfect example of an obedient, faithful servant. This is a love that any Christian wife can have for her husband even if he does not love her as he should. God will give her grace.

The second kind of love that a wife is to have for her husband is *philos* love. This kind of love is thinking of your husband as the father of your children or thinking of him as your husband who works hard at his job so that he can pay the bills for your family. This kind of love of a wife for her husband is what the older women are to teach and train younger women to have (Titus 2:3–5).

The third kind of love is *eros* love. We get our English word "erotic" from this Greek word. It is sexual love. This is an area in your lives that should be mutually enjoyed and unselfishly given to the other as long as what you are doing is not sinful. (For more on this topic, see chapter 18.)

The vow taken at your wedding to love "till death do you part" is not intended to be the empty, forgotten words of a beautiful ceremony and a sweet tradition. It is a biblical mandate to be lived out over a lifetime together as you sacrifice for, have sexual relations with, and cherish your husband. The love that God requires is not one of warm, fuzzy feelings but an act of your will as you turn more and more from unloving thoughts and actions such as selfishness, fear, or bitterness to loving your husband as God intended.

QUESTIONS FOR REFLECTION AND APPLICATION

- Do you think more about what you can do for your husband or what he can do for you?
- Are you patient with your husband?
- Do you sometimes play hurts over and over in your mind, or are you quick to forgive?
- Is your tone of voice kind and gentle, or is it harsh or sarcastic?
- Do you ever punish your husband by pouting or giving him the cold shoulder if you do not get your way?
- Do you save some time and energy for your husband each day?
- Are you affectionate?
- What are your husband's top three wants? Can you fulfill them?

- ❧ What are some ways that your husband would like for you to show love to him?
- ❧ Do you try to think of ways to show love to your husband, such as preparing his favorite meal or writing him a sweet note?
- ❧ Do you treat your husband as someone special in public and when it is just the two of you at home?

FAVORITE RESOURCES

Martha Peace. *Becoming a Titus 2 Woman.* Bemidji, MN: Focus Publishing, 1997.

Elyse Fitzpatrick. *Helper by Design.* Chicago: Moody Publishers, 2003.

Lord,

Marriage is ordained by you. It is holy and good.

You have given a wife the responsibility to love her husband by self-sacrifice, cherishing him, and intimacy with him.

You also grant those who know you the grace to obey with a joyous heart.

It truly is a sacred trust.

May my desire to love and cherish my husband be greater and more mature than it was on the day we married.

Help me to truly love my husband in a way that would be pleasing not only to him but also to you, Lord.

In Jesus' name,

Amen.

8

Husbands Leading the Way

There is no command in the Bible for husbands to lead their wives. "What?" you may exclaim. Of course there is, and probably more than one! If you think that is true, you are reading your Bible quickly, not carefully. Slow down as you look at the verses. Ephesians 5:22–24 says, "Wives, submit to your own husbands, as to the Lord. For the husband is the head of the wife even as Christ is the head of the church, his body, and is himself its Savior. Now as the church submits to Christ, so also wives should submit in everything to their husbands."

The other place where the man's position in the home is found is in 1 Corinthians 11:3, which says, "But I want you to understand that the head of every man is Christ, the head of a wife is her husband, and the head of Christ is God."

Although these two passages clearly indicate that the husband is the head of the wife, neither commands him to lead her. It is always an assumed fact that you are responsible for the well-being of your family. The only question is, what kind of head are you?

Whether or not you have been well-taught on your role, whether or not your wife is a spiritually-minded woman, whether or not you feel adequate to do the job, you are ultimately going to be called to account by the Lord for your life as well as how you led your wife. No excuses will do on that day. God has called you to this role, and he will give you the grace to exercise your headship in a way that is pleasing to him.

When I was in seminary, I built a bookcase in the living room of our apartment. We may never know how much sawdust got into that carpet. Special projects can be accomplished under less than ideal circumstances, but a garage or a workshop would've made for a much better environment to do the job. In a similar way, God has designed men and women to function most effectively within their roles. Otherwise, marriage can be messy. In other words, you need to lead your wife for your family to be all that God designed it to be.

Your wife needs you to lead her. For example, you should be the one to initiate being more involved at church. You patiently walk through her weekly schedule and help her establish priorities and goals. You show her by example how to faithfully walk with God when your own schedule is crying for mercy. Don't try to justify not leading her by coasting on her spirituality. Excel as the godly leader that God has made you.

QUESTIONS FOR REFLECTION AND APPLICATION

- ❧ What is your wife's spiritual condition?
- ❧ Are you watching her spiritual diet? What is she learning in the Bible? favorite books? preaching? tapes or radio?
- ❧ What is your game plan to help her get where she needs to be spiritually?
- ❧ Do you complain when things in your home go wrong?
- ❧ Are you the initiator in general and specifically regarding the means of spiritual progress such as church involvement and family worship?
- ❧ Do you use the word "let's" more than she does?
- ❧ Are you working hard at making wise decisions (prayer, searching the Scriptures, asking wise friends, even taking the time to write out the pros and cons)?
- ❧ Do you respond to your wife when she asks for help?
- ❧ Do you accept responsibility when you choose to go along with her decision?
- ❧ Are you setting an example of walking with the Lord?
- ❧ What are some of the dangers you are trying to protect your wife from (harmful influences from books or other media, or even a close friendship with an ungodly woman)?

FAVORITE RESOURCES

Stuart Scott. *The Exemplary Husband.* Bemidji, MN: Focus Publishing, 2000.

John Crotts. *Mighty Men.* Sand Springs, OK: Grace and Truth Books, 2004.

What a great God you are!

You made the heavens and the earth; you made the family.

While some days I may not feel like I've got what it takes to lead my wife and children, you appointed me to the task.

Give me strength to be a man.

Give me grace to be a wise and godly leader.

Help me to lead in such a way that I make you smile and make the world take notice of how Jesus leads his church.

Amen.

9

Biblical Submission, the Wife's Joy

Recently, the state of Louisiana experienced a horrific hurricane that caused the levees to break and the city of New Orleans to flood. Thousands of people were stranded and in desperate need of rescue. On the Saturday following the storm, at 6:30 a.m., the helicopters arrived. They landed one at a time with the next one waiting in the air to land as soon as the previous one was airborne. Due to training of the helicopter pilots and their rescue crews, their maneuvers were in perfect harmony with one another. They were flying people out at the rate of one hundred people every ten minutes, and that effort stopped only after they had evacuated thousands of people. It was an incredible sight to behold. It was made possible only by the pilots' training to submit to the orders of those in command. There were no power plays. The pilots knew their roles, and they executed them flawlessly.

Biblical submission of a wife to her husband is similar. Both husband and wife are to know their roles and live them out under the overriding authority of the Lord. For the wife, that means she is to obey her husband in all things unless her husband asks her to sin. Even though this subject is greatly misunderstood in the world and in the church, the biblical command of the wife to submit to her husband is clear (Eph. 5; Col. 3; Titus 2; 1 Peter 3). Often it is easier to understand what is meant by submission through considering what biblical submission is not. Then we will see what it is.

Submission does not mean that the wife is inferior to her husband. In fact, she may be superior in many ways. She simply has a different role to fulfill within the marriage. Also, submission does not mean that she is to obey her husband if he asks her to sin. God is always the higher authority, and his commands override anyone's sinful mandates.

Submission does not mean that the wife should never express her opinion or her desires. However, she should be willing to defer to her husband's wishes if his way is important to him. Additionally, submission does not mean that she is to be a doormat and never say anything no matter how her husband treats her. And finally, submission does not mean that she is off the hook in regards to submission if her husband is an unbeliever.

Submission does mean that the wife is to obey in all things unless her husband asks her to sin (Eph. 5:22–23). The Greek word for obey is *hupotasso,* and it is a military term that means to be ranked under in military order. Within marriage, ranking was determined by God for his glory.

Submission also means that a submissive wife "[does] good and [does] not fear anything that is frightening" (1 Peter 3:6). She shows love to God by obeying his Word, and it is more important for her to obey the Lord than to have her own way. Her hope is in God, and she is not given to fear and worry but instead trusts God. Submission also means that the wife does not dishonor the Word of God because her priority is obedience to God instead of having her own way (Titus 2:5).

A submissive wife is letting the Word of Christ direct her life instead of sinfully giving in to her emotions or her selfish heart. Therefore, she is submissive whether she feels like it or not. Like the rescue crews of the helicopters who undoubtedly got great satisfaction from a job well-done, a submissive wife (because she loves the Lord) is biblically submissive to her husband. That is her joy.

QUESTIONS FOR REFLECTION AND APPLICATION

- ❧ When you appeal to your husband to have your way, what is really more important to you—having your way or pleasing God?
- ❧ Would your husband say you nag him in order to have your way?
- ❧ Do you graciously take no for an answer?
- ❧ Do you ever think or say to your husband, "I would like to . . . , but whatever you decide is fine with me," and you mean it?
- ❧ Do you ever pout or brood when you do not get your way?

- Is it easy for your husband to express his opinion, or is he afraid to tell you what he really thinks?
- Can your husband trust you to do as he has asked even when he is not around or is out of town?
- Do your children look to you or to their father as the head of the home?
- How would you explain what the word *hupotasso* means?
- Is it your joy to be under your husband's authority because you know that pleases the Lord?

FAVORITE RESOURCES

Martha Peace. *The Excellent Wife.* Bemidji, MN: Focus Publishing, 1995.

John MacArthur. *Different by Design.* Wheaton, IL: Victor Books, 1994.

Dear Lord Jesus,

We are reminded that you did not demand to have equality with the Father when you came to earth.

You carried out the plan of salvation perfectly.

You did it for the joy that was set before you.

Lord, we live in a world where equal rights has become a god.

Our hearts demand that we have our way.

Give me your heart, Lord, that as a wife I will not resent the role you have given me.

Make righteous submission to my husband my joy.

In your holy name I pray,

Amen.

10

Living According to Knowledge

D. Martyn Lloyd-Jones, the famous medical doctor turned preacher in London during the mid-twentieth century, used to give this advice, "Know yourself." Each person is different; what works for one must not be assumed to be universal. This is true about everything from differing amounts of sleep or exercise needed per day to a person's specialized temptations and remedies. In addition to Lloyd-Jones's prescription to know ourselves, the Bible charges men with the doubly difficult responsibility of knowing our wives. Peter is clear about this: "Likewise, husbands, live with your wives in an understanding way, showing honor to the woman as the weaker vessel, since they are heirs with you of the grace of life, so that your prayers may not be hindered" (1 Peter 3:7).

The idea of this command is to live with your wife "according to knowledge." Of course, this means that we should appreciate the differences between men and women in general. The applications, however, seem to extend to an intimate understanding of what specifically makes your wife tick. Each woman is unique, so your job is to be a lifelong student at the University of Your Wife! She is a special creature made by God and has been entrusted especially to you. He expects you to work hard at this task.

In calling her "the weaker vessel," Peter has in mind the vulnerability of a precious vase. While it is true that generally women are physically weaker than men, this fact is not usually viewed as an honorable thing. You must honor your wife because she is like fine china or a rare jewel. Handle her with honor and with great care.

The seriousness of this command is seen in the final phrase, "so that your prayers may not be hindered." If you are routinely harsh, selfish, negative, or critical with your wife, not only will you have an upset wife, but also you will build a wall between you and her heavenly Father. In a sense, this verse is saying that because she is a fellow Christian, God is your spiritual father-in-law. If you do not carefully study your wife and treat her with respect, when you come knocking on God's door with your prayers, he will turn you away. This charge is serious business!

Questions for Reflection and Application

- Are you an active student of your wife?
- Do you regularly ask your wife questions to mine the treasures of her heart?

❧ Are you sensitive to the differences between you and your wife?

❧ What are your wife's strengths? What are her weaknesses? What are some of her toughest temptations?

❧ What is her weekly schedule? Are her duties being accomplished in the most efficient ways?

❧ When is she most likely to feel overwhelmed? When is she most tempted to become overwhelmed?

❧ What is one way you can relieve her of a burden?

❧ Are there unfinished projects around the house that your wife would love for you to tackle? Make a plan to accomplish them, and ask her to prioritize them. If possible, tackle them according to her priorities.

❧ Do you appreciate that God custom-designed your wife for you?

❧ What are ten things about your wife that you thank God for?

❧ Does your wife know that you value her? (You'd better ask her, just to be sure!)

❧ In what ways does she most feel loved by you?

❧ Your wife is unique; think of seven specific ways to communicate your love and respect for her that she would appreciate. Do one of these each day for a week.

FAVORITE RESOURCES

Lou Priolo. *The Complete Husband.* Amityville, NY: Calvary Press, 1999.

Alistair Begg. *Lasting Love.* Chicago: Moody Press, 1997.

As David said, Father, "O LORD, you have searched me and known me! . . . You search out my path and my lying down and are acquainted with all my ways. Even before a word is on my tongue, behold, O LORD, you know it altogether" (Psalm 139:1, 3—4). Father, I need to know my wife more as you know me. She is so precious but so very different from me.

Her position is different, as you have called her to follow my lead, and she is different in being a wonderful and unique woman. Yet she is exactly the same in that we are both one of your children. Seeking to appreciate and balance these differences and similarities can be overwhelming. But then, you already knew that about me! Help me to be faithful.

In Jesus' name,

Amen.

II

Respecting Your Husband

In Paul's magnificent section on marriage in Ephesians 5, he compares Christ's relationship to the church with the relationship of the husband to his wife. The section ends with "and let the wife see that she respects her husband" (Eph. 5:33). Respect is often shown in the little ways, such as your tone of voice, how you look at your husband, or how you speak about him to others.

Respect is to be given to your husband's position as head in the home (1 Cor. 11:3). So, whether the husband deserves it or not, the wife is to show respect to him because it is due him. It is especially important when it is necessary for a wife to tell her husband that what he is doing is not right that she always reprove him with a respectful tone and manner.

Suppose you had the opportunity to talk to the governor of your state. And suppose he is trying to get the legislature to enact more liberal abortion laws. What would you say to him, and how would you say it? If you do not show respect to the governor and to his position, you won't get very far. Scripture says that if you want to influence someone, "sweetness of speech increases persuasiveness" (Prov. 16:21). It is the same with your husband. Whether your husband honors God and loves you as he should or not, you are to heed the biblical mandate, "Let the wife see that she respects her husband" (Eph. 5:33).

QUESTIONS FOR REFLECTION AND APPLICATION

- Do you treat your husband in private as respectfully as you do your pastor, neighbor, or friend in public?
- Do you speak to your husband in a kind, gentle tone or a sarcastic, condescending tone?
- Do you show disrespect by sighs, angry looks, looks of disgust, or crossed arms?
- Do you talk for your husband or interrupt him?
- Do you try to intimidate or bully your husband by making threats, verbally attacking him, crying, or in some other way manipulating him to have your way?
- Do you bring up your husband's shortcomings to others?
- Do you contradict your husband in front of others?
- Do you listen carefully to your husband's opinion, trying to understand him?
- Do you respect his requests by trying to do as he asks, even if it does not seem important to you?

❧ Do you respect his position in the home so much that he can depend on you to do as he asks even when he is not home?

❧ Are you kind and loving in your tone of voice, or are you harsh in tone?

❧ Are you obeying God by being respectful to your husband?

FAVORITE RESOURCES

Matthew Henry. *The Quest for Meekness and Quietness*. Morgan, PA: Soli Deo Gloria Publications, 1996. (originally published 1698)

Wayne Mack. *Anger and Stress Management, God's Way*. Merrick, NY: Calvary Press, 2004.

Almighty God,

You are the only one who can tame the tongue.

You are the only one who can give us a desire to even try.

You are the only one who has never responded in sinful anger or sarcasm.

You are my perfect example.

My request is that you will convict me when I am disrespectful to my husband.

Help me to faithfully show respect to my husband whether I feel like it or not.

In Jesus' name I pray,

Amen.

12

The Husband Provides for the Home

Does your wife know that your family has its needs met? Can she rest tonight knowing that beside her is a man who owns up to his responsibility to provide for his home? While every family experiences temporary setbacks and even job transitions, a godly man will be a faithful provider for his family. "But if anyone does not provide for his relatives, and especially for members of his household, he has denied the faith and is worse than an unbeliever" (1 Tim. 5:8).

There are at least three major lessons for a husband fulfilling his responsibility to provide for his family. The first two are taught by an unlikely professor.

Go to the ant, O sluggard;
    consider her ways, and be wise.

Without having any chief,
>   officer, or ruler,
she prepares her bread in summer
>   and gathers her food in harvest.
How long will you lie there, O sluggard?
>   When will you arise from your sleep?
A little sleep, a little slumber,
>   a little folding of the hands to rest,
and poverty will come upon you like a robber,
>   and want like an armed man. (Prov. 6:6–11)

Lesson one is to be a hard worker. In contrast to the hard-working ant, the sluggard is a bump on a log. The sluggard loves sleep and is a master of justifications and excuses. All he provides for his family is poverty, even though the Bible is clear about a man's responsibility to be a diligent worker.

Paul charges the Thessalonians "to aspire to live quietly, and to mind your own affairs, and to work with your hands, as we instructed you, so that you may live properly before outsiders and be dependent on no one" (1 Thess. 4:11–12). In another letter to this same church, he adds, "For you yourselves know how you ought to imitate us, because we were not idle when we were with you, nor did we eat anyone's bread without paying for it, but with toil and labor we worked night and day, that we might not be a burden to any of you. . . . For we hear that some among you walk in idleness, not busy at work, but busybodies. Now such persons we command and encourage in the Lord Jesus Christ to do their work quietly and to earn their own living" (2 Thess. 3:7–8, 11–12).

If you are between jobs, your job is to get a job! Although it is not wrong to be in transition, it is wrong to piddle around hoping your next job will fall in your lap. Also, be realistic. If you want to start your own business and do not have the startup money, it may be best to get a steady, paying job while you start your business on the side.

Lesson two from the ant (Prov. 6) is to plan for the future. Just as the ant works in the hot summer to save supplies for the bleak winter, so you must work to make sure your family will have what it needs for those days when you will no longer be able to work. Wisdom is needed to balance necessary savings against the sinful practice of hoarding, and that leads to the third lesson.

Lesson three goes after your heart: It is better to sacrifice stuff than your family. Many men want their wives to work outside of the home, or they work a second job or excessive hours so the family can have more stuff. Beware of greed! Notice the boundaries of contentment that Paul lays out in 1 Timothy 6:8: "But if we have food and clothing, with these we will be content."

In the first century, architecture and clothing were meager compared with the typical lifestyles of today. So when Paul says we should be content with food, clothing, and by application adequate shelter, he does not mean fifteen or twenty changes of clothes per season, ten pairs of shoes, and a twenty-five-hundred-square-foot home on a one-acre lot. It is not a sin to have things if you are living within your means, but it is a sin if those things have you. What do you really need?

Most Christians who go on a short-term mission trip confess that it affected them far more than anything they did for the people they visited. It is usually shocking to Americans to see just how good they have it materially. Seeing how fellow Christians live around the world should be a help in realigning our priorities.

So yes, work hard to provide for your family. Do plan ahead for emergencies and retirement. But always check your heart against the sins of greed and hoarding. A good solution to these sins is to give away plenty of money.

QUESTIONS FOR REFLECTION AND APPLICATION

- Compared with those around you, how is your productivity at work? How is it compared with what it could be?
- Are you a wise worker, looking for opportunities to get better at what you do?
- Should you be positioning yourself to open a new career pathway to better provide for your family?
- Are you disciplined to save money each month?
- Do you freely give money to your church and to meet other worthwhile needs?
- Are you able to meet your family's budget by your own earnings?
- What are some examples of where you and your wife may confuse needs and greeds?
- Are you trusting the Lord for real needs that seem to be going unmet (Matt. 6:33)?
- Are your family priorities being overshadowed by your job(s) or by your wife working outside of the home?

FAVORITE RESOURCES

John Crotts. *Craftsmen.* Wapwallopen, PA: Shepherd Press, 2006.

Mark Chanski. *Manly Dominion.* Merrick, NY: Calvary Press, 2004.

You are the ultimate Provider of all things in life.

You meet my family's needs, and you fill our lives with good gifts to enjoy.

I look to you, O God, to care for my family.

While I look to your providing hands, make my hands work hard to faithfully serve you as I serve my family.

As you give to me through my occupation, make my hands hold onto my things loosely.

Help me and my family to give freely as we have freely received from you.

Amen.

13

The Wife Sets the Tone in the Home

When I was a little girl, I remember my mother singing and dancing around the room and twirling me around with her. One time she taught me how to do a dance that the flappers in the 1920s were famous for. The name of the dance was the Charleston. There was a lot of joy for both of us in those moments. Because of my mother's mood at the time, my little girl's heart was full of joy.

In a similar way, the everyday, ordinary Christian life of a wife should be one of joy and fulfillment in honoring God and serving him. The godly wife "laughs at the time to come" and has "the teaching of kindness . . . on her tongue" (Prov. 31:25, 26). Family members in her home don't have to wonder, "What kind of mood is Mama in?" Because she sets a warm, loving tone in her home, she looks forward to life and to what the Lord is going to do.

The tone in the home is set not only when there is joy in the Lord but also when the home is clean and organized. Since the wife is to be a worker at home, she should be good at keeping house. This can mean making a menu and grocery list and grocery shopping once per week, or keeping up with the laundry so there is no chaos on Sunday morning with each family member running around trying to find a matching pair of socks. Being organized also helps greatly during the times when a wife is providentially hindered by sickness; consistent organization means that everything hasn't fallen into such disrepair that she'll never catch up on her work.

Probably the best summary describing a wife who sets a godly, joyful tone in her home is that she has a "gentle and quiet spirit" (I Peter 3:4). Having a gentle and quiet spirit does not mean a woman whispers when she talks. It does mean that she accepts God's dealings with her as good and that she is not given to anger or fear. She's humble, teachable, and delighted to obey God and serve her family. She works hard, is good at what she does, and, as we said earlier, "laughs at the time to come" (Prov. 31:25). And because of her joyous tone, everyone else in the home will be laughing, too.

QUESTIONS FOR REFLECTION AND APPLICATION

- Is your home more like a peaceful retreat or more like a war zone?
- Are you more likely to think, "This makes me mad!" or "What might God be doing in this situation?"
- Which describes how you would likely react—sighing

and withdrawing in anger or in gentleness trying to help the other person understand?

❧ Are you more likely to play angry thoughts over and over in your mind or likely to give the other person a blessing by praying for him or her?

❧ Do you enjoy life and love life, or do you dread each day and fret and worry?

❧ Are you easily provoked or slow to anger?

❧ Are your thoughts calm and rational, or do you sometimes overreact to circumstances?

❧ Do you forebear (put up with others), or are you easily provoked for small cause?

❧ Do you use anger and threats to manipulate those under your authority, or do you give instruction in love?

❧ Do you err on the side of mercy when correcting those under your authority, or are you harsh?

❧ Do you grumble and complain at your present circumstances that disappoint you, or are you grateful to God for what he is doing?

❧ Do you delight in the Lord and trust him? Is that obvious to others?

❧ Is your home reasonably clean?

❧ Is your home organized or chaotic?

❧ Do you have a good sense of humor?

❧ Is there a ready smile on your face?

❧ What kind of tone do you think you set in your home? What would your family say?

FAVORITE RESOURCES

Pat Ennis and Lisa Tatlock. *Becoming a Woman Who Pleases God.*
 Chicago: Moody Publishers, 2003.
Pat Ennis and Lisa Tatlock. *Designing a Lifestyle That Pleases God.*
 Chicago: Moody Publishers, 2004.

Lord,

It is your kindness that draws us to you.

It is your promises to us that cause us to look forward to each day.

You are consistent, and we can depend upon you. We do not have to dread what kind of mood you may be in.

When we think of how you are, it gives us great joy.

Help me to be like you in the tone that, by your grace, I set in my home.

Thank you for the work you have given me to do and for my family.

In your name I pray,

Amen.

RESPONSIBILITIES

14

Communication

My brothers, these things ought not to be so." (James 3:10). James is referring to the words that come out of our mouths. How sad that "from the same mouth come blessing and cursing" (James 3:10). Tragically, it is possible to be mature in many areas of our Christian walk, but when it comes to what we say, we often fall short.

Because we all fall short and may especially be tempted to communicate sinfully to our spouse, we all need to pay careful attention to how God wants us to communicate. In general, we are to speak truthful words in love accompanied by appropriate mannerisms and a kind tone of voice. These kinds of words are edifying and give grace to the hearer (see Eph. 4:29). More specifically, our words are to show that we are to give each other the benefit of the doubt. In other words, do not negatively judge your spouse's motive (Matt. 7:2; 1 Cor. 4:5). That will prevent you from overreacting emotionally and being overly sensitive.

If you know your spouse has something against you, go immediately to him or her and try to reconcile the matter (Matt. 5:24). Be quick to listen, and do not answer until the other person has finished speaking (Prov. 18:13; James 1:19). Do not be hasty to answer, but stop and think first. Speak in a calm, gentle tone. It is especially important when you are wrong that you admit it and ask forgiveness. Also, ask how you should change (James 5:16; Prov. 12:15).

Do not use the "silent treatment" to punish the other person. When you do, you are being immature and cruel. Also, be aware that it is the fool who responds in uncontrolled anger. No matter what the disagreement with your spouse, it is always possible for you to honor God whether your spouse does or not. Try to understand each other's opinion, and always make allowances for differences. It helps greatly to consider your spouse as more important than yourself (Phil. 2:3).

God-honoring communication is an area in which we all struggle. Work hard at this biblical discipline, and the Lord will help you be forbearing, edifying, and loving. Remember that you communicate not only with your words but also with your tone of voice and how you look at your spouse. Any violation of one of these three areas of communication is a sin against God and your spouse. The bad news is "these things ought not to be so." The good news, though, is that in Christ, it doesn't have to be that way.

Questions for Reflection and Application

❧ What areas of strength regarding communication do you think you have? What areas of strength do you think your spouse has?

- What areas of weakness regarding communication do you think you have? What areas of weakness do you think your spouse has?
- Do you make an effort to talk to your spouse? in other words, to share your life? How many minutes do you typically spend talking to your spouse each day?
- Do you pay attention to what your spouse is trying to tell you, or have you already made up your mind about what he or she is going to say?
- Are you hasty and hurtful with your words, or do you carefully think about what you should say?
- Are you sarcastic, or do you make fun of your spouse?
- Are you an interrupter?
- Are you willing to let your spouse hold you accountable for your areas of weakness?
- What practical things could you do to help each other recover once sinful communication begins? (For example, signal with a gentle pat on the arm, or suggest you stop talking and pray.)

FAVORITE RESOURCES

Wayne Mack. *Strengthening Your Marriage.* Phillipsburg, NJ: P&R Publishing, 1977; 2nd ed., 1999.

Paul David Tripp. *War of Words.* Phillipsburg, NJ: P&R Publishing, 2000.

Lord Jesus,

You are the living Word of God, and you have communicated with us through your Word, the Scriptures.

Your Word is true, and we are sanctified in it.

It is the means by which we learn to communicate with each other in a righteous way.

By your grace and through your Word, we learn how to speak loving and edifying words to each other.

Being completely dependent on your mercy and grace, my request is that you will "let the words of my mouth and the meditation of my heart be acceptable in your sight, O LORD, my rock and my redeemer" (Ps. 19:14).

Amen.

15

Facing Trials Together

*E*very relationship comes with trials. Whether you are just getting to know each other or have been married for fifty years, you will experience tough times. Sometimes the trials are because both of you are sinners, and sinners sin against each other. Other times you will experience other tests, such as an unexpected budget buster, a car crash, or random family members offering not-so-helpful ways for you to run your lives.

The most essential help in responding to any trial in a way that honors the Lord is to frame the trial biblically. As you step back and look at the trial, whatever it is, you must bring God into your thinking. Almost every fight, angry reaction, stressful overload, or anxiety attack is caused by practical atheism. You may say you believe the right things about God and the Bible, but when you react to trials as if God doesn't exist, you are a practical atheist.

God certainly does exist. He is completely sovereign over each and every trial. If you are a Christian, he is at work in and around the trial for your good and his glory. He will never let you be tempted beyond what you are able to bear. He will always give you the grace to honor him as you endure the trial. Since every couple is rocked by trials at different levels at various times, all of us need to work hard at framing our understanding of trials biblically so that we can respond rightly to them.

James 1:2–5 is the first of three power passages in helping you frame your trials in a God-honoring way: "Count it all joy, my brothers, when you meet trials of various kinds, for you know that the testing of your faith produces steadfastness. And let steadfastness have its full effect, that you may be perfect and complete, lacking in nothing. If any of you lacks wisdom, let him ask God, who gives generously to all without reproach, and it will be given him."

The only way that you can consider a trial to be joy is good theology! By faith you have to remind yourself that God is in this thing. Not only that, he is working in it to produce Christian maturity in you and your spouse. Even then, the Bible packs in that promise that if we don't have the wisdom to be joyful in our hardships, we can ask God for help, and he will answer us.

The second power passage is Romans 8:28–30: "And we know that for those who love God all things work together for good, for those who are called according to his purpose. For those whom he foreknew he also predestined to be conformed to the image of his Son, in order that he might be the firstborn among many brothers. And those whom he predestined he also called, and those whom he called he also justified, and those whom he justified he also glorified."

It is not enough to stop at the often memorized Romans 8:28, which says all things are working for good. The next two verses explain the meaning of that good. God is producing Christlikeness in his children through every event in their lives. It is fair to say that if you are a Christian, you have been put on a course from before you were born that includes chipping off all of the rough edges to make you like Jesus. Although this doesn't mean that everything you experience in life is good, it does mean that God is working everything you experience toward his glory and your good.

The final power passage to aid couples in framing their trials in a godly way is 1 Corinthians 10:13: "No temptation has overtaken you that is not common to man. God is faithful, and he will not let you be tempted beyond your ability, but with the temptation he will also provide the way of escape, that you may be able to endure it."

Your trials are never unique; they are common to man—or common to couples! Your trials are never unbearable. Your trials are never inescapable. When you are tempted to doubt any of the statements above, remember 1 Corinthians 10:13. The truth of God's Word is a powerful antidote to the lies of the flesh and the devil.

Don't let your relationship suffer because of practical atheism! You must first of all honor the Lord in the midst of your trials. But your relationship will be revolutionized as you begin to do this as a couple. We will all face trials, but we don't have to be toppled by them. By God's grace, we can triumph through them.

Questions for Reflection and Application

❧ What are some recent examples of trials you have experienced? trials faced together or trials caused by each other?

- How long does it usually take to bring God into your thinking?
- Which one of you usually begins thinking like a Christian first?
- Do you encourage one another that even though you don't know what will happen, God does, and he will help you both go through the trial?
- Do you add to your spouse's burden or make it as easy as you can for him or her?
- Are there times when either one of you uses Scripture inappropriately during your trials?
- When under stress do you take it out on one another through anger or withdrawal?
- Do you overreact?
- Do you jump to the worst possible conclusion or panic?
- Can you count your blessings when you find yourself in a trial?
- Do your friends at church point you to God or sing the blues with you in hard times?
- Do you see the connection between faith and a godly response to trials?
- What are some ways you can help each other bring God into your thinking?
- Do you pray about difficult circumstances together?
- Do you remind yourself and your spouse of God's goodness and thank him for what he is teaching you?

FAVORITE RESOURCES

Jay Adams. *Christ and Your Problems.* Phillipsburg, NJ: P&R
  Publishing, 1971.
Jerry Bridges. *Trusting God.* Colorado Springs, CO: NavPress,
  1988.

Our marriage seems so easy when everything is going well, Father.

But you ordain every trial that interrupts our ease. You are working in thousands of ways in each event.

Please help us remember that.

Help us respond to the trials and to each other in the midst of the trials in a way that shows we believe in you and are grateful to you!

Please forgive us for the times we have acted as if you didn't exist.

Get glory for yourself by making us more like Jesus using whatever means that you deem best.

Because of the mercy of Jesus,

Amen.

16

Conflict Resolution

There can be a hundred toys in the room with two toddlers. The toys can all be bright, shiny, fun, and age-appropriate for them. Imagine that the toys are scattered equally around the room and the children are placed in the middle of the room and left to play. Then the drama begins! It matters not which toy is picked up first or who picks it up. It is a universal truth that the other child will want the same toy. The ensuing mayhem will not be resolved until an adult intervenes.

Usually the adult's question is, "Who had this toy first?" By that time, it doesn't matter, because both children are angry and screaming at the top of their lungs. Both are being sinful and selfish, and they don't care about solving the conflict. Some adults are like that, but all adults can learn by God's grace to solve any kind of conflict in a way that honors the Lord and shows love to their spouse.

Conflict can occur over a righteousness issue, a different-ness issue, or a selfishness issue. An example of a righteousness conflict is when one spouse thinks it is fine to look at pornography and the other does not. A differentness conflict occurs when one spouse wants to paint the living room yellow and the other wants to paint it green. Selfishness conflicts occur when the husband plays golf every spare minute that he is not at work or the wife pays the bills and has money only for what *she* wants to purchase. Regardless of the underlying cause of the conflict, though, there is always a biblical solution.

When the conflict is over a righteousness issue, the answer is whatever Scripture dictates. The offending spouse who thinks it is acceptable to look at pornography must repent and "make no provision for the flesh, to gratify its desires" (Rom. 13:14). If he or she does not repent, then his or her spouse must follow the guidelines covering church discipline (Matt. 18:15–18). This would be very difficult for both husband and wife, but at least one of them would be upholding God's high and holy standard.

When the conflict is over differentness, listen carefully and lovingly to each other's view. Try to determine if a compromise could be reached or if seeking counsel (in this case, decorating counsel) would help you come up with a color that you both might like. The husband should want to please his wife, but ultimately, the wife will need to be graciously, biblically submissive to her husband because choosing a wall color is not asking her to sin.

When the conflict is caused by selfishness, the selfish one must repent. If you confront your spouse's selfishness, be sure to give clear, concrete examples. If he or she disagrees with you, together seek wise counsel so that a third person can make a biblical assessment determining whether there is a problem with selfishness or not.

There is no problem, however large or small, that cannot be solved biblically, for God has granted believers "all things that pertain to life and godliness" (2 Peter 1:3). Conflicts are to be addressed using biblical communication in a God-honoring way. There is no sin that cannot by God's grace be repented of and no relationship conflict that cannot be reconciled if both persons are willing to humble themselves and proceed in a righteous manner. It takes work to solve problems biblically, but the result of glorifying God has the promise of eternal reward as well as blessings in the here and now in your marriage.

QUESTIONS FOR REFLECTION AND APPLICATION

- ᛜ When is the last time you and your spouse had a conflict?
- ᛜ Was the conflict due to righteousness, differentness, or selfishness?
- ᛜ Was there anything that you did wrong during the conflict?
- ᛜ Was there anything else you think your spouse did wrong besides what he or she has already mentioned in the previous question?
- ᛜ If you could go through the conflict again, what would you do differently?
- ᛜ When you have conflict, do you stick to the issue at hand or do you bring up the past?
- ᛜ Do you speak the truth in a loving tone?

- Do you try to understand your spouse's viewpoint?
- Is it more important to you to show love or to have your own way?
- Is it more important to you to glorify God or to have your own way?

FAVORITE RESOURCES

Ken Sande. *The Peacemaker.* Grand Rapids: Baker, 2004.

Jay Adams. *Solving Marriage Problems.* Grand Rapids: Zondervan, 1983.

Heavenly Father,

We are reminded of the worst possible conflict, the personal conflict we have with you because of our sin.

There is only one resolution, and that is the death of your Son on the cross.

You are the all-powerful, holy God who poured out your wrath on your beloved Son, so that we may have peace with God and the supernatural peace of God.

Because of what you have done for us, those of us who believe can, at least, have the potential to solve conflict with others and not sin.

Grant us humility, gentleness, patience, and love with each other so that we may maintain the unity that you desire and that we may glorify you, our Father in heaven.

Amen.

17

Money Matters in Marriage

Money is so important in a marriage. We are stewards of all that God has entrusted to us. We must make enough money to support our families. Money can be a tool to enhance our marriage through thoughtful gifts of flowers or a needed vacation. Money also provides opportunities to serve the Lord by giving together to the church, the needy, and in the support of missions.

Money is so unimportant in a marriage. You don't need nearly so much money to have a happy home. While some couples work feverishly to have nice things, other couples have discovered the truth of Proverbs 15:17, which says, "Better is a dinner of herbs where love is than a fattened ox and hatred with it."

God has given each one of us our money. He uses it in our lives to test us. Often, money reveals what is in our hearts. Our priorities are displayed by our checkbook or credit card statements. When couples are tested by money, money is not the problem, even when it is lacking—the character of the couple is what is being examined. Hidden structural flaws within the marriage are discovered by financial hardships.

The Bible is the resource the Lord has given couples to direct all areas of their lives. The financial arena is no exception to the rule. Although space is quite limited in this chapter to exhaust the subject—the Bible says more about money than it does about heaven and hell combined—let's consider a few reminders.

All of your money belongs ultimately to the Lord, and he has entrusted what you have to you as a steward. Since it is his money loaned to you, you are to use your resources for his glory. In Psalm 50:10, God reminds us that "every beast of the forest is mine, the cattle on a thousand hills." Everything in your wallet and garage is God's!

While the application is broader, 1 Corinthians 4:7 speaks of God giving us all of what we have. "For who sees anything different in you? What do you have that you did not receive? If then you received it, why do you boast as if you did not receive it?" Although couples often assume that they are completely free to use their money in any way that they please, they are not. What God has given to you is to be used as he intends.

Out of that general truth come several subsequent truths. Trust God for your provisions. How many couples fight with each other in reaction to anxiety they feel over how the bills are going to be paid? Instead of glaring at each other, look to the Lord for your daily bread. "But seek first the kingdom of

God and his righteousness, and all these things will be added to you" (Matt. 6:33).

Strive to be generous. Planning for the future is wise (Prov. 6:6–8), but hoarding is sinful. It is okay to enjoy the good things the Lord has provided (1 Tim. 4:4), but how many professing Christians do you know who are drunk on materialism? "As for the rich in this present age, charge them not to be haughty, nor to set their hopes on the uncertainty of riches, but on God, who richly provides us with everything to enjoy. They are to do good, to be rich in good works, to be generous and ready to share, thus storing up treasure for themselves as a good foundation for the future, so that they may take hold of that which is truly life" (1 Tim. 6:17–19).

Have a budget. If I came over this evening, would you be able to show me your working budget? Would it represent all of the money you are responsible for in the month? Are you and your spouse on the same page as to the budget category amounts? Are you both striving to stay within every category? If you don't have a budget and follow it, do you know how much of the Lord's money you are squandering? Couples who learn how to use a budget not only are better stewards of the Lord's money but also enjoy spending it, because they know they are using it responsibly.

Beware of credit cards. They can be useful tools, but many, many couples get sucked down the drain as they live beyond their means and then can't keep up with the credit-card payments. The interest on some credit cards is more than 20 percent. Minimum payments at those rates are a recipe for financial ruin. If that is where your family is . . . STOP! Repent for any and all foolish spending. Cut up the cards. Start living on a budget and within your means. Blast away at the debt, and refuse to add to it. Don't go shopping except for basic necessities; otherwise you will find something you didn't know existed and be tempted to buy it impulsively. Get help and accountability from godly leaders at your church.

Set financial goals. As you discuss your family's financial situation as husband and wife, take time to set some savings goals. These goals can be spiritually oriented, such as saving to support a mission trip. Or, they can be for a special trip for the two of you. It is also important to have an emergency fund available.

Even though husbands are responsible for the overall welfare of the home, including the finances, wives are custom-designed by God to help the men out. A wife's input into the planning and implementing of the family budget is important. Both the husband and the wife will be better and happier stewards of the Lord's resources if both parties' input has been considered.

Money doesn't have to be a problem in a marriage, but it does have to be thought about and handled biblically. Money is a test that can be passed with flying colors as couples seek to honor God with their resources. Keep in mind, "But if we have food and clothing, with these we will be content" (1 Tim. 6:8).

Questions for Reflection and Application

- Do you have a clear perspective on the fact that God owns all of your resources?
- How are you treating his money?
- How much money have you given away lately?

❧ Do you have a working budget?
❧ Does your budget accurately reflect all that you are responsible for?
❧ Have both spouses participated in making that budget?
❧ Do you ever carry a balance on your credit cards?
❧ What is your plan to eliminate debts, especially credit-card debt?
❧ Do you have financial goals?
❧ Are you trusting God for your finances?
❧ Who would you go to for help in organizing your finances?

FAVORITE RESOURCES

Ron Blue. *The New Mastering Your Money.* Chicago: Moody Press, 2004.

Randy Alcorn. *The Treasure Principle.* Sisters, OR: Multnomah, 2001.

Father, money tests our marriage.

Sometimes we do so well in handling all of the resources that you have entrusted to our care, but other times we fail.

Our greed is revealed, along with our carelessness and thoughtlessness.

May our checkbooks cry out, "Glory to God," as they are balanced each month. May our credit cards praise you, because we have used them as a tool to advance your kingdom.

May our budget discussions be times of worship and gratitude, celebrating your goodness and the grace you have given us to be faithful stewards.

Amen.

18

Sex

There is now more information available on the subject of sex than ever before. There are technical manuals and "how to be romantic" books. There are secular books and Christian books on the topic. There are legal books and illegal books on the topic. Everyone has an opinion about sex. There are now doctors who specialize in it, and there is even a supposed disease named for it—sexual addiction. It is almost impossible to tune into a television station without being bombarded by the subject of sex. With all this information readily available, you would think that everyone is well-informed, somewhat of an expert, and free of problems in that area of their marriage. However, that is not the case. Sex is often a cause of conflict or hurt feelings between husbands and wives.

Although any problem that a couple has should be discussed in love while God's wisdom is being sought, sex, ironically, is often a subject that is avoided like the plague. Sex in marriage is supposed to be righteous and glorify God. It is a gift given to couples for their enjoyment and for procreation. But, like any skill, physical love between a husband and wife has to be learned and practiced for one to become good at it. Practice and good communication do make perfect!

Physical intimacy should be a loving act with a husband and wife seeking to please the other. Neither should try to impose sinful desires on their spouse, and this includes gray areas that would violate the wife's or husband's conscience to participate. Instead, each spouse should be pure before the Lord in this area and "let marriage be held in honor among all, and let the marriage bed be undefiled" (Heb. 13:4).

In order to be pure before the Lord, each spouse is to keep himself or herself (as the traditional marriage vows say) "only unto themselves." In other words, they should be faithful not only outwardly but also in their hearts. That means that neither should entertain romantic or sexual fantasies about others. It will help if neither husband nor wife makes any provisions for their flesh, such as pornography, sensual movies, soap operas, or romance novels (see Rom. 13:12–14).

Neither spouse should deprive the other of physical intimacy. Either one can and does have the authority and responsibility to initiate sex (1 Cor. 7:3–5). Therefore, sex should be a regular part of married life so that each spouse is satisfied and not unnecessarily struggling with desire. When a couple is apart due to illness, the husband's job, or other circumstances, then self-control becomes the guiding biblical principle.

Remember that sex between husband and wife is to glorify God and to be a blessing to both husband and wife as they seek to show love to the other.

QUESTIONS FOR REFLECTION AND APPLICATION

- ❧ Do you save time and energy to have sex with your spouse?
- ❧ Are you clean and do you smell good when you come together?
- ❧ Do you graciously take no for an answer if your spouse expresses distaste for or sinful concern about a particular act?
- ❧ When engaging in the act of love, do you concentrate on what would please your spouse?
- ❧ Wives, do you talk to your husband and tell him how to be a good lover to you?
- ❧ Husbands, do you talk to your wife and tell her how to be a good lover to you?
- ❧ Do you have a problem with sexual lust?
- ❧ What can your husband or wife do that would make it easier for you not to be tempted to lust?
- ❧ Do both husband and wife feel free to initiate sex?
- ❧ If either is being providentially hindered, do you make good on your rain checks?
- ❧ Are you having regular sexual relations, or do you live together more like brother and sister?

FAVORITE RESOURCES

C. J. Mahaney. *Sex, Romance, and the Glory of God: What Every Christian Husband Needs to Know.* Wheaton, IL: Crossway, 2004.

Ed Wheat and Gaye Wheat. *Intended for Pleasure.* Old Tappan, NJ: Revell, 1977.

Our pure and holy God,

You have set your high and holy standard for physical intimacy in marriage.

You have given it to us as a gift to enjoy.

Help us to be true to each other not only outwardly but also in our hearts.

Help us to not be selfish but loving and freely giving to each other.

May we use this sacred trust you have given us in a way that would glorify you.

In Jesus' name,

Amen.

19

Parenting

hildren are a blessing from the Lord, and they bring a lot of joy into any home with their laughter and play. They also bring a lot of responsibility to the parents. Of course, parents are supposed to feed their children, protect them, and keep them clean; but additionally, they have a much more important responsibility. That responsibility is to "bring them up in the discipline and instruction of the Lord" (Eph. 6:4).

As precious as children naturally are, they are not born loving God and loving others. They are born, however, loving one person dearly—themselves! Folly is bound in their hearts, and they are sinners from birth (Prov. 22:15). What's a parent to do? The answer is "bring them up in the discipline and instruction of the Lord" each and every day. One way is for Mom and Dad to model a godly Christian life in front of their children. Otherwise, they will be unnecessarily provoking their children to anger (Eph. 6:4; Col. 3:21).

The model of your life is only one way to instruct them in the Lord. Other ways are faithful attendance at Sunday school and church, fellowship with other believers, family devotions, and prayer. Parents must learn to think biblically before they can, in turn, instruct their children. For example, the parents should teach their child to think in terms of biblical love. "Son, I want you to sit quietly and wait while I finish cooking dinner. This is a way you can show love to me because the Bible teaches that 'love is patient' " (1 Cor. 13:4).

In addition to modeling your life and instructing your child, parents are to discipline their children. The short-term goal is for your children to graciously obey the first time you instruct them while you are speaking in a normal tone of voice. Discipline in love, and do not overreact. For the younger child, it usually means a spanking; for the older child, a work penalty or restriction. The long-term goal is for your child to submit himself to God. Of course, only God can save your child, but meanwhile you can give your children the gospel and pray for their salvation.

When giving the gospel to your child, be aware that merely asking Jesus into your heart is not the gospel. Tell them the truth—God is holy and you are a sinner. Because you are a sinner, you deserve to be punished for your sin. The Lord Jesus Christ, God in the flesh, came to earth and died on the cross for our sins. In other words, he took the punishment that we deserve. The Bible tells us that we cannot save ourselves, but we can ask God for mercy, and to forgive us, and save us. The Scriptures say, "Believe in the Lord Jesus, and you will be saved" (Acts 16:31). You will want to teach them these things and more. Continue to plant little seeds of truth as you go through life with them.

Parenting is a great joy, and children are a blessing from God. Enjoy your children and work together to "bring them up in the discipline and instruction of the Lord" (Eph. 6:4).

Questions for Reflection and Application

- ❧ Are you consistent with discipline?
- ❧ Is one or both of you too hard on the children?
- ❧ Is one or both of you too lax in your discipline?
- ❧ Do you usually agree on the type and severity of the discipline?
- ❧ Do both parents take initiative with discipline?
- ❧ Do you both talk to the children about the Lord?
- ❧ Are you faithful to take the time to instruct the children in the Lord?
- ❧ Can you think of some examples where you can do a better job with the children?
- ❧ Do you know how to give the gospel to your child?
- ❧ What are each child's strengths and weaknesses?
- ❧ What can you do to help your children with their weaknesses?
- ❧ What can you do to help your children enhance their strengths?

Favorite Resources

Tedd Tripp. *Shepherding a Child's Heart.* Wapwallopen, PA: Shepherd Press, 1995.

Elyse Fitzpatrick and Jim Newheiser. *When Good Kids Make Bad Choices.* Eugene, OR: Harvest House, 2005.

Heavenly Father,

Children are a blessing from you.

Your Word gives us much instruction about how to raise them up.

You also warn us not to provoke them to anger.

May we be like you, Father, instructing them with great patience and disciplining them with great love.

May you grant our children salvation so that they can give you honor and glory.

In your name we pray,

Amen.

Martha Peace was born, raised, and educated in and around the Atlanta area. She graduated with honors from both the Grady Memorial Hospital School of Nursing and Georgia State University. She has thirteen years' experience as a registered nurse, specializing in pediatric burns, intensive care, and coronary care.

She became a Christian in June of 1979. Two years later, Martha ended her nursing career and began focusing attention on her family and a ladies' Bible study class. For five years she taught verse-by-verse book studies. Then she received training and certification from the National Association of Nouthetic Counselors. NANC was founded by Jay E. Adams for the purpose of training and certifying men and women as biblical counselors. (For more information, visit www.nanc.org.)

Martha is a gifted teacher and exhorter. She worked for eight years as a biblical counselor at the Atlanta Biblical Counseling Center, where she counseled women. For the past several years, she has presented a workshop on various biblical counseling issues for women at NANC's annual conference. She also taught women's classes for six years at Carver Bible Institute and College, in Atlanta. Currently, Martha is a member of the adjunct faculty at The Master's College, in Valencia, California, teaching biblical counseling. She has authored five books: *The Excellent Wife*, *Becoming a Titus 2 Woman*, *Attitudes of a Transformed Heart*, *Damsels in Distress*, and *Tying the Knot Tighter*.

Martha is active with her family in Faith Bible Church in Peachtree City, Georgia, where she teaches a ladies' Sunday school class, sings in the choir, counsels women, and generally serves where needed. In addition, she conducts seminars for ladies' groups on topics such as "Raising Kids without Raising Cain," "The Excellent Wife," "Becoming a Titus 2 Woman," "Having a High View of God," and "Personal Purity." She speaks at a number of women's conferences each year both nationally and internationally.

Martha has been married to her high school sweetheart, Sanford Peace, for forty-one years. He is an air traffic controller with the FAA, but his real work is as an elder at Faith Bible Church. They have two married children and ten grandchildren.

John Crotts is the pastor-teacher of Faith Bible Church in Sharpsburg, Georgia. He holds degrees from Liberty University and The Master's Seminary and serves as a board member of FIRE (Fellowship of Independent Reformed Evangelicals). John has written *Mighty Men: The Starter's Guide to Leading Your Family* and *Craftsmen: Skillfully Leading Your Family for Christ.* He and his wife Lynn have been blessed with three daughters and a son: Charissa, Danielle, Chloe, and Josiah.

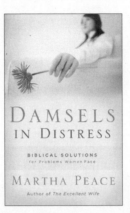
"Several years ago I was introduced to Martha Peace through her book *The Excellent Wife*. I remember then saying, 'This is the best book I've ever read on the topic of the wife. Martha deals with real issues that wives face and offers real biblical solutions.' *Damsels in Distress* is also a book about real problems with real biblical solutions. This is a must for women who are struggling with deep-rooted sin and for women who desire to help other women to live victoriously in Christ Jesus."

—SUSAN J. HECK, author of *With the Master in the School of Tested Faith*

"*Damsels in Distress* clearly reveals God's principles for dealing with the common problems women face—first with others, then with themselves. Through its pages you will be stimulated to honestly analyze the problems through the grid of Scripture and then formulate practical applications that bring glory to God."

—PAT ENNIS, professor, The Master's College, author of *Precious in His Sight* and *The Fine Art of Becoming a Godly Woman*

"In *Damsels in Distress* Martha exhorts her readers to an uncompromising standard of personal holiness. The chapters on the interpersonal sins of gossip and manipulation should be especially helpful for women who struggle with temptations to sinful speech."

—LAURA HENDRICKSON, M.D., biblical counselor and co-author of *Will Medicine Stop the Pain?*

RELATED RESOURCES FROM P&R

To order, visit
www.prpbooks.com
or call
1(800) 631-0094

"In whatever state you see your own marriage, I am confident you will find here the principles and practices you've searched for as you seek to reflect Jesus Christ's relationship to His bride—the church."

—LANCE QUINN, president, National Association of Nouthetic Counselors

"*Sweethearts for a Lifetime* roots marriage in Christ and the gospel, and in separate sections devoted to men and women it identifies the callings God has clearly given them in Scripture. This book bears reading and rereading by couples together!"

—TEDD TRIPP, pastor, author, conference speaker

"Christian marriages are meant to get better over time. It is for want of knowing and applying the truths Wayne Mack has spelled out so well in this book that many marriages do not."

—MARTIN HOLDT, pastor, Constantia Park Baptist Church

RELATED RESOURCES FROM **P&R**

To order, visit
www.prpbooks.com
or call
1(800) 631-0094

For *better* or for *worse*? Whichever term describes your marriage, there are ways to make it (even) better. That's because God has designed marriage to be a relationship of deep unity and strength. Despite the challenges that couples face today, marital harmony need not be considered an impossible ideal.

Wayne A. Mack recognizes the challenges before us, and shows us how to meet those challenges with growing success. In this book, he has gathered a wealth of biblical insight and practical information on marital roles, communication, finances, sex, child rearing, and family worship. Both as a counseling aid and as a guide for husbands and wives to study together, this book offers true hope and help where couples need it most.

RELATED RESOURCES FROM P&R

As a husband, father of four, and family counselor, Wayne A. Mack knows what makes families tick. Here he offers biblical insight and practical wisdom into two crucial areas of family life: communication and conflict resolution. Alerting us to the pitfalls of faulty communication, such as "undertalk," "overtalk," poor listening, forms of falsehood, and "circuit jammers" to communication, Mack examines why families fight and explains the key to turning family discord into harmony.

Firsthand success stories and highly practical application questions give hope and clear direction to all who wish to build stronger families God's way.

RELATED RESOURCES FROM P&R

To order, visit
www.prpbooks.com
or call
1(800) 631-0094

"From his years of counseling experience, Lou Priolo has developed a work that exposes many of the prideful manifestations of people-pleasing, while also walking the reader through the biblical process of repentance from the heart. This is a book that God can use greatly to change lives."

—STUART SCOTT, associate professor of biblical counseling,
The Southern Baptist Theological Seminary

"Lou Priolo has written an extremely biblical and practical book to help the 'people-pleaser.' Even if you think you do not have this weakness, you may be convicted that you do! The strengths of this book are its biblical principles, its charts with wrong compared to right ways of thinking, and its counsel on how to become a 'God-pleaser.' I am very pleased to have this resource for helping people, and I highly endorse it."

—MARTHA PEACE, biblical counselor and author of
The Excellent Wife and *Damsels in Distress*

"Lou has done a great job in unmasking the problem of people-pleasing and providing God's solution to the problem. I commend this book to you because of its biblical and extremely practical nature. Buy it, read it, reread it, and use it in your counseling and teaching."

—WAYNE MACK, director of Strengthening Ministries

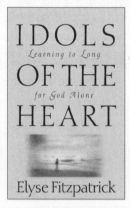